Foreword

2020 started as strange year that continued to astonish. In Australia, we battled bushfires, endured the floods that the draught and in some places witnessed plagues of locusts. It was biblical. But no one could be prepared for what came next. There was talk of a bad flu in China. It didn't take long for Covid-19 to reach us.

In the early days of autumn something else happened. Vito started writing poems.

It started as an SMS dialogue, but the words kept coming. In many respects, Vito's poetry could be known as the "Covid Diaries'. His poems are responses that come to Vito in his everyday life. They have become an externalised version of what lives inside Vito's head.

His stimulus comes from al angles, as wide ranging as a Fellini movie, the taste of coffee or the look from a stranger in the street.
The poems come at all times of the night and day. Vito regularly wakes up at 3:00am with a poem in his head that has to escape. This diversity of subject matter reflects the multi-faceted diamond which is the mind of "The Don".

Mariclare Pringle
November, 2020

Contents

1: Mind Games
(Giochi Mentali)
2: Believe
(Credere)
3: Children of the Universe
(Figli dell'Universo)
4: Ripples in Time
(Increspature nel Tempo)
5: What's the Name of the Game?
(Qual è il Nome del Gioco?)
6: Live Your Life
(Vivi la tua Vita)
7: Poem for Non-Poets
(Poesia per Non-Poeti)
8: The Secret to a Happy Life
(Il Segreto per una Vita Felice)
9: No Expectations
(Senza Aspettative)
10: I Hate Shakespeare
(Odio Shakespeare)
11: In Your Garden
(Nel tuo Giardino)
12: Emotions
(Emozioni)
13: Forever Young
(Per Sempre Giovani)
14: Mythologise
(Mitologizzare)
15: Insanity
(Follia)
16: Lay with Me
(Sdraiti con Me)

Acknowledgement of Land & of the Traditional Owners of this Land

I would like to acknowledge the Gadigal people of the Eora Nation, upon whose stolen land I stand on today.

I recognise that this land was never terra nullius — the land belonging to these peoples was never ceded, given up, bought or sold.

I would like to pay my respects to Aboriginal Elders past, present and emerging, and I extend this acknowledgement to all Aboriginal and Torres Strait Islander people.

"The Don"
Artist: Daniela Dali

VOICE. TREATY. TRUTH.
ULURU STATEMENT FROM THE HEART

We, gathered at the 2017 National Constitutional Convention, coming from all points of the southern sky, make this statement from the heart:

Our Aboriginal and Torres Strait Islander tribes were the first sovereign Nations of the Australian continent and its adjacent islands, and possessed it under our own laws and customs. This our ancestors did, according to the reckoning of our culture, from the Creation, according to the common law from 'time immemorial', and according to science more than 60,000 years ago.

This sovereignty is a spiritual notion: the ancestral tie between the land, or 'mother nature', and the Aboriginal and Torres Strait Islander peoples who were born therefrom, remain attached thereto, and must one day return thither to be united with our ancestors. This link is the basis of the ownership of the soil, or better, of sovereignty. It has never been ceded or extinguished, and co-exists with the sovereignty of the Crown.

How could it be otherwise? That peoples possessed a land for sixty millennia and this sacred link disappears from world history in merely the last two hundred years?

With substantive constitutional change and structural reform, we believe this ancient sovereignty can shine through as a fuller expression of Australia's nationhood.

Proportionally, we are the most incarcerated people on the planet. We are not an innately criminal people. Our children are aliened from their families at unprecedented rates. This cannot be because we have no love for them. And our youth languish in detention in obscene numbers. They should be our hope for the future.

These dimensions of our crisis tell plainly the structural nature of our problem. This is the torment of our powerlessness.

We seek constitutional reforms to empower our people and take a rightful place in our own country. When we have power over our destiny our children will flourish. They will walk in two worlds and their culture will be a gift to their country.

We call for the establishment of a First Nations Voice enshrined in the Constitution.

Makarrata is the culmination of our agenda: the coming together after a struggle. It captures our aspirations for a fair and truthful relationship with the people of Australia and a better future for our children based on justice and self-determination.

We seek a Makarrata Commission to supervise a process of agreement-making between governments and First Nations and truth-telling about our history.

In 1967 we were counted, in 2017 we seek to be heard. We leave base camp and start our trek across this vast country. We invite you to walk with us in a movement of the Australian people for a better future.

This consensus followed a ground-breaking process First Nations from across Australia through 12 deliberative dialogues. Joining each dialogue were a representative sample of approximately 100 Indigenous people drawn from local traditional owners, Indigenous community-based organisations and Indigenous leaders. These regional dialogues selected their own representatives to attend the First Nations Constitutional Convention at Uluru. At the Convention, and by an overwhelming consensus, more than 250 delegates adopted the Uluru Statement.

A First Nations Voice to Parliament.
The voice to parliament would be a representative body giving Aboriginal and Torres Strait Islanders a say in law and policy affecting them. Enshrined in the constitution, it would become an institution of lasting significance for First Nations and all Australians.

Contents

17: I Will Listen
(Ascolterò)
18: Yowie Woman
19: She's the Girl from Rio, Rio de Janerio
(Ela é a Menina de Rio, Rio de Janerio)
20: Money
21: Queen Sheila
22: Laughter is the Name of the Game
(La Risata è il Nome del Gioco)
23: The Wonderful Land of Oz
24: Night Time
(la Notte)
25: I'm a Failure
(Sono un Fallimento)
26: Lo♥e Sick
(Amore Malato)
27: Karma
28: Why Do You Have to Make Relationships Work?
(Perché Devi Far Funzionare le Relazioni?)
29: If You Can't Play with Somebody Else, Play with Yourself!
(Se Non Puoi Giocare con Qualcun Altro, Gioca con te Stesso!)
30: The Muse
31: I Must've Done Something Wrong
(Devo aver Fatto Qualcosa di Sbagliato)
32: Yes
(Sì)
33: Abused
(Abusata)
34: Your Eyes
(I tuoi Occhi)
35: Unrequited Lo♥e
(Amore non Restituito)

Contents

36: I Woke Up with a Hard On
(Mi Sono Svegliato con Un'erezione)
37: I Give Up
38: Your Tribe
39: It is What it is
(È Quello Che è)
40: You need Lo❤e
(Hai Bisogno di Amore)
41: The Girl with the Large Labia Lips
(La Ragazza con le Grandi Labia Labbra)
42: You Got Something to Say?
(Hai Qualcosa da Dire?)
43: The Witching Hour
(L'ora delle Streghe)
44: She's in Control
(Ha il Controllo)
45: I'm in Deep
(Sono In Profondità)
46: A Cry
(Un Piangere)
47: You're a Fascist!
(Sei un Fascista!)
48: Equilibrium
(Equilibrio)
49: I Am
(Io Sono)
50: I'm Not Going to Sleep with You!
(Non Vado a Letto con Te)

Mind Games

(Giochi Mentali)

You take life too seriously.
You gotta lighten up.
You gotta see the positive side of things.
You gotta walk on the sunny side of the road.

Life is but a game.
Life is but a joke.
Life is but a riddle.
Life is but ride.

It's all one big mind fuck.
It's all one big mind meld.
It's all one big mind bender.
It's all one big mind game.

We all do it.
We're all to blame.
We all know the rules.
We all play the game.
We all try to outdo each other.
We all try to cheat to win the game.
We all try to break the rules.
We all know the name of the game.

Winners are grinners.
The winner gets it all.

There are no prizes for second best.
There are no prizes if you fall.
There are no prizes for trying your best.
There are no prizes giving it your all.
There are no prizes being kind.
There are no prizes on how you play the game.

Take no prisoners.
Show no mercy.
Win at all cost.
Fuck the rest.
Glory is your reward.
Untold riches is what you deserve.
A bevy of beauties will share your bed.
You will be wined & dined until you are fed.

This is you reward.
This is your prize.
This is what you are playing for.
This is what you live for.
This is what you struggle for.
This is what you fight for.
This is what you compete for.
This is what you battle for.
This is what you LIVE for.
This is what you DIE for.

Do you have the strength?
Do you have the fortitude?
Do you have the gumption?
Do you have the will power?
Do you have the strength of character?
Do you have the strength of mind?
Do you have what it takes to play?
Do you have what it takes to win?
The Mind Games!

Mind Games

"The Don"
18.08.2020

Believe

(Credere)

Believe in *me*.
Believe in *you*.
Believe in *beauty*.
Believe in *happiness*.
Believe in *joy*.
Believe in *purity*.
Believe in *passion*.
Believe in *desire*.
Believe in *creativity*.
Believe in *innocence*.
Believe in *respect*.
Believe in *compassion*.
Believe in *friendship*.
Believe in *caring*.
Believe in *kindness*.
Believe in *goodness*.
Believe in *positivity*.
Believe in *optimism*.
Believe in *Science*.
Believe in *energy*.
Believe in *amazing*.
Believe in *awesome*.
Believe in *Future*.
Believe in *Life*.
Believe in *feelings*.
Believe in *sensuality*.
Believe in *sexuality*.
Believe in *eroticism*.
Believe in *art*.
Believe in *music*.
Believe in *culture*.
Believe in *fascination*.
Believe in *curiosity*.
Believe in *imagination*.
Believe in *Lo♥e*.
Believe in *Humanity*.
Believe in *yourself*.
Believe.

"The Don"
19.08.2020

Children of the Universe

(Figli dell'Universo)

You are made of "Star stuff".
You are made from "Light".
You are made from "The Cosmos".
You are made from "Sun".
You are made from "Plasma".
You are made from "Anti-Matter".
You are made from "Dark Matter".
You are made from "Nebulae".
You are made from "Solar flares".
You are made from "Interstellar gases".
You are made from "Cosmic forces".
You are made from "Cosmic Energy".
You are made from "Cosmic Frequency".
You are made from "Cosmic Vibrations".
You are made from "Cosmic Electromagnetic Waves".
You are made from "Polarity".
You are made from "Duality".
You are made from "Thought".
You are made from "Thinking".
You are made from "Feeling".
You are made from "Dreams".
You are made from "Space-Time".
You are made from "Lo♥e".
You are made from the "Darkness".
You are made from the "Heavens".
You are made from the "Dreaming".
You are made from the "Big Bang".
You are made from the "Multiverse".
You are made from the "Universe".

You are a child of the Universe!

"The Don"
19.08.2020

Ripples in Time

(Increspature nel Tempo)

Where are we going?
What is our destination?

Do we have a map?
Do we have a plan?
Do we have a compass?
Do we have a guide?
Do we have a path?
Do we have a road?
Do we have food?
Do we have water?
Do we have a long way to go?
Do we know our way?
Do we have an end?
Do we know where to stay?
Do we know when we get there?
Do we know if we've arrived?

Will our actions be enough?
Are we doing the right things?
Could we do it much better?
Do we know anything?
Is there a sign that can help us?
Is there an arrow to show us the way?
Is there a clearly defined path?
Or do have find our own way?

What about if I get lost?
What will happen to me then?
Will I be missed?
Will anyone ever know that I'm not there?
Will someone come & search for me?
Will I be out in the cold?
Will be all alone?
All by myself?
With no one to help me?
I get scared & lonely in the dark!

I don't like to close my eyes.
I don't like to sleep in the dark.
I don't like to get lost.
I like know where I'm going.
I like to know where I'm headed.

I live in quiet desperation.
I am a desperate Lo♥er.
I hear the silent voices shouting.
I hear their cries in the darkness.
I hear them in the stillness of the night.
I hear them but no one else can.

Only I can hear them.

Ripples in Time

"The Don"
29.08.2020

What's the Name of the Game?
(Qual è il Nome del Gioco?)

Are we playing a game?
How come I wasn't told?
What are the rules?
What the name of the game?

Is it "Game of Thrones"?
With its intrigues & subterfuge.
Is it "Game of Cards"?
With its political backstabbing & treachery.
Is it "Five Card Stud"?
Is it "Blind Man's Bluff"?
Is it "Strip Poker"?
Is it "Spin the Bottle"?
Is it "Snakes & Ladders"?
Is it "Backgammon"?
Is it "Checkers"?
Is it "Chess"?
Is it "Football"?
What's the name of the game?

Does it have a name at all?
Do we make up the rules as we go?
How do we score any points?
Where are there goalposts?
Where is there a try line?
How do we score a "touch down"?
Is there a referee?
Is there an "out of bounds"?
Is there a "time out"?
Are there any "subs"?
Can I start on the "bench"?
What's the name of the game?

How long does it go for?
Is it played in quarters or in halves?
How many reserves are allowed?
What happens if you're injured?
Is there a medical doctor?
Should I have trained for it?
Will I get paid?
What's the name of the game?

Can I have sex before the game?
Is that allowed?
Who is the coach?
Is this a team game?
Or am I all alone?
Can I have a partner?
Can I ring a friend?
What's the name of the game?

What's this all about anyway?
Is this the beginning or the end?
Has the game already started?
Shit, why wasn't I told?
Was that the final whistle?
Has the game come to an end?
How did I do?
Will I be picked again?
When will I be told?
Will I be waiting a long time for an outcome?
Is it a score out of ten?
What's the name of the game?

What's the Name of the Game?

"The Don"
19.08.2020

Live Your Life

(Vivi la tua Vita)

Do not live with fear.
Do not live with regrets.
Do not live with missed opportunities.
Do not live with unhappiness.
Do not live with sadness.
Do not live with commitments.
Do not live with obligations.
Do not live with compromises.
Do not live with hatred.
Do not live with violence.
Do not live with abuse.
Do not live with disrespect.
Do not live with emptiness.
Do not live with Death.

Live your life with happiness.
Live your life with joy.
Live your life with tenderness.
Live your life with beauty.
Live your life with adventure.
Live your life with fun.
Live your life with humour.
Live your life with passion.
Live your life with risks.
Live your life with chances.
Live your life with emersion.
Live your life with integrity.
Live your life with principles.
Live your life with honour.
Live your life with innocence.
Live your life with sensuality.
Live your life with kindness.
Live your life with caring.
Live your life with respect.
Live your life with compassion.
Live your life with friendship.
Live your life with Lo♥e.
Live your life with Life.

You only have one life.
So, live it well.
Live it full.
Live it completely.
Live your life.

"The Don"
20.08.2020

Poem for Non-Poets

(Poesia per Non-Poeti)

Don't like poetry?
Think that poetry's for wimps?
Think that poetry's for nerds?
Poetry's not your thing?
Then this poem is for you.

Everyone is a poet.
You just don't know it.
You've been told you're no good.
You had a bad time a school.
Words don't come easily to you.
You're the "strong, silent type".
Well, think again.
You're a poet & you don't even know it.
You can make a rhyme anytime.

We all have thoughts.
We all have ideas.
We all have feelings.
We all have desires.
We all have wants.
We all have passions.
We all have emotions.
We all have regrets.
We all have failings.
We all have dreams.
We all have nightmares.
We all have fears.

These are the things poems are made of.
Just write them down.
Get them out of your head.
Put them down on paper.
Don't worry about how it's written.
Don't worry if it doesn't rhyme.
It doesn't matter.
What matters is that it's yours.
Just let it "flow".
Let yourself go.
Let it all out.

Don't listen to others.
Don't listen to other people's opinions.
Don't overthink it.
Don't be critical.
Don't be analytical.
Don't be worried about what others might think.
Don't be worried about what words to use.
Don't be worried about if it's "any good".
Don't be worried about whether people will like it or not.
Don't be worried about anything.
Don't CENSOR yourself!

You're doing it for yourself.
That's all that matters.
Everyone's a poet.
Even if you think you are not.

Poem for Non-Poets

"The Don"
20.08.2020

The Secret to a Happy Life
(Il Segreto per una Vita Felice)

In my experience with Lo♥e, you take what you get!
That's it!
If you want more, you will be unhappy!
Just accept the situation & move on with your life.

Have many relationships at one time.
Do not try to possess anyone.
You NEVER will!

Just do your own thing & be happy within yourself!
If someone wants you, they will come to you.
The attraction is in NOT being needy!
In being INDEPENDENTLY happy!

That is the SECRET to a happy life.

"The Don"
21.08.2020

No Expectations

(The Secret to Happiness)
Senza Aspettative
(Il Segreto della Felicità)

Do not seek.
Do not pursue.
Do not persuade.
Do not convince.
Do not manipulate.
Do not contrive.
Do not plan.
Do not pre-plan.
Do not bedazzle.
Do not construct.
Do not coerce.
Do not stalk.
Do not control.
Do not plead.
Do not beg.
Do not need.
Do not chase.
Do not pine.
Do not grovel.
Do not cry.
Do not fear.
Do not guilt.
Do not agonise.
Do not panic.
Do not stress.
Do not fear.
Do not theorise.
Do not define.
Do not ruminate.
Do not cogitate.
Do not prepare.

Do not hypothesis.
Do not theorise.
Do not rehearse.
Do not predict.
Do not assume.
Do not overthink.
Do not formulise.
Do not organise.
Do not solidify.
Do not quantify.
Do not regiment.
Do not constrain.
Do not restrain.
Do not mould.
Do not project.
Do not impose.
Do not restrict.
Do not contain.
Do not imprison.
Do not confine.
Do not enchain.
Do not shackle.
Do not fetishise.
Do not force.
Do not pressure.
Do not compare.
Do not impress.
Do not expect.

The Secret to Happiness is: Do not have Expectations!

"The Don"
21.08.2020

I Hate Shakespeare
(Odio Shakespeare)

I never really liked him.
All that "old English" language.
I was never really impressed.
It was all so contrived.
There were no real emotions.

His comedies weren't really funny.
His tragedies weren't really tragic.
His romances weren't really romantic.
His histories weren't really historic.
His thrillers weren't really thrilling.

"To be or not to be?"
That's all I can remember.
Hamlet, "Spamlet".
What a wimp of a character.
His existential crisis my arse.

Pathetic Juliet.
What a loser.
Falling for that daggy Romeo.
And then killing themselves over Lo♥e.
Why didn't they just run away!

Ophelia was another loser.
Othello was not much better.
Shylock with his "pound of flesh", another loser.
They were all pathetic characters.

Tell me the truth.
Admit to me here.
No one else will know.
No one will read this anyway.
I bet you hate Shakespeare too.

"The Don"
21.08.2020

In Your Garden
(Nel tuo Giardino)

What do you have planted in your garden?
Have you recently planted some "*Despair*"?
What about "*Frustrations*"?
They always grow very well.
And they proliferate easily & quickly
If they are allowed to grow unchecked.

I'm sure you've got some "*Fear of Failure*" growing somewhere?
This can hang around for a very long time.
Possible hidden in the undergrowth.
In the back of the garden.
In a corner, maybe?
Out of sight but not inactive.
Spreading its roots & it's tentacles unnoticed for years even.
Until one day it blossoms into all its glory.
It's actually a climber & it should never be planted.
But people don't really know or care that much.
About what they plant in their garden.

Another beautiful but dangerous plant is "*Hatred*".
It has very dark purple flowers with a pungent smell.
Whatever you do don't touch it.
Its leaves have a furry underbelly that is poisonous to Humans.
But is completely safe for animals.
Strange how Nature works?

Of course, who can forget "*Anger*"?
It's almost like a "*Boganvilia*" in shape & growth.
With huge thorns & beautifully coloured, delicate flowers.
Don't let this one, get out of control.
Because it starts growing will take over.
It will spread throughout your garden
Suffocating everything else.
You'll have to get professional help to remove this "*motherfucker*".
Believe me, I've had this happen to me.
Cost me a pretty penny to get it removed.
And it's never really totally gone.
Years later there are new shoots growing.
It just doesn't seem to able to be killed.

Fuck, there's some "*Cruelty*", "*Abuser*" & "*Exploitation*" growing as well.
These 3 are part of the "*Deadly NightShade*" family.
As the name suggests, they grow undercover of the night & are very deadly.
Get rid of them immediately.
The recommended method is to burn them.
Burn every tiny leaf.

May I suggest you plant some "*Respect*", "*Compassion*", "*Friendship*" & "*Lo❤e*".
These are known as the "*Ghia-EarthMother*" family.
Just to balance your garden out.

So, have you checked what's in your garden lately?

"The Don"
22.08.2020

Emotions

(Emozioni)

Emotions are a two-edged sword.
Emotions can take you to Heaven.
Emotions can take you to Hell.
Emotions can you to the euphoric heights of Pleasure.
Emotions can take you to the depths of Despair.
Emotions can unify you with the Cosmos.
Emotions can dismember you into the Abyss.
Emotions can shine a light on your Path.
Emotions can darken your your Journey.
Emotions can be your Salvation.
Emotions can be your Destruction.
Emotions can make you Free.
Emotions can make you a Prisoner.
Emotions can be your Friend.
Emotions can be your Enemy.
Emotions can be Liberating.
Emotions can be Suffocating.
Emotions can be Ecstatic.
Emotions can be Dramatic.
Emotions s can be Beautiful.
Emotions can be Ugly.
Emotions can make you Lo♥e.
Emotions can make you Hate.
Emotions can give you Life.
Emotions can give you Death.
Emotions can make you Human.
Emotions can make you Inhuman.
Emotions can be Controlled by You
Emotions can Control You.
Emotions can be Possessed by You.
Emotions can Possess You
Emotions can be Used by You.
Emotions can Use You.
Emotions can be Decided by You.
Emotions can Decide You.
Emotions can be Chosen by You.
Emotions can Choose You.

It's your decision.
You decide.
We ALL have Emotions.
There is no denying that.

So, it up to you.
Whether you let your Emotions control you.
Or, *you control you Emotions*.

"The Don"
23.08.2020

Forever Young

(Per Sempre Giovani)

Everyone ages.
Everyone gets old.
Everything decays.
There is no denying it.
There is no escaping this.
Accept it.
Don't fight it.
We are all going to die.
Eventually.
Stay "*Forever Young*".

But remember one thing.
It's all in your head.
Yes, your body ages.
But, your "Mind" doesn't have to.
If you don't let it.
Stay "*Forever Young*".

Stay young in your *Mind*.
Stay young in your *Thoughts*.
Stay young in your *Ideas*.
Stay young in your *He♥rt*.
Stay young in your *Soul*.
Stay young in your *Kindness*.
Stay young in your *Caring*.
Stay young in you *Being*.
Stay young in your *Humanity*.
Stay young in your *Lo♥ing*.
Stay "*Forever Young*".

Never give *Up*.
Never give *In*.
Never stop *Thinking*.
Never stop *Feeling*.
Never stop *Caring*.
Never stop *Lo♥ing*.
Never *Stop*.
Stay "*Forever Young*".

"You're as old as the person you're feeling!"
Feel Young.
Think Young.
Stay Young.
Be Young.
In your *Mind*.
Never *get old*.
In your *Mind*.
Stay "*Forever Young*".

"Mind over Matter!"
"You are what you think!"
That's what they say.
So, think Young.
And you'll NEVER get old.
Not where it matters.
In your Mind & in your He♥rt.
Stay "*Forever Young*".

"May God bless and keep you always
May your wishes all come true
May you always do for others
And let others do for you
May you build a ladder to the stars
And climb on every rung
May you stay forever young
May you stay forever young

May you grow up to be righteous
May you grow up to be true
May you always know the truth
And see the light surrounding you
May you always be courageous
Stand upright and be strong
May you stay forever young
May you stay forever young

May your hands always be busy
May your feet always be swift
May you have a strong foundation
When the winds of changes shift
May your heart always be joyful
May your song always be sung
And may you stay forever young
May you stay forever young."

"Forever Young" Songwriter: Bob Dylan

"The Don"
24.08.2020

Mythologise

(Mitologizzare)

Create your own *Myth*.
Create whom you *wanna be*.
Create your own *Story*.
Mythologise.

Create your own *Ideas*.
Create what you want to *Think*.
Create what you want to *Feel*.
Mythologise.

Create your own *World*.
Create your own *Universe*.
Create your own *Cosmos*.
Mythologise.

Create your own *Dreams*.
Create your own *Hopes*.
Create your own *Future*.
Mythologise.

Create *yourself*.
Create yourself *many times*.
Create many *versions of yourself*.
Mythologise.

Create your own *Lo♥ers*.
Create your own *Life*.
Create your own *Death*.
Mythologise.

Create your own *Rebirth*.
Create your own *Paradise*.
Create your own *Heave*n.
Mythologise.

Mythologise *Yourself*.
Mythologise your *Life*.
Mythologise your *World*.
Mythologise.

I am a *Myth*.
I am a *Mythical Myth*.
I am a *Mythology*.
Mythologise.

"The Don"
25.08.2020

Insanity

(Follia)

Insanity is everywhere.
Insanity is the air.
Insanity is the water.
Insanity is the food.
Insanity is in Families.
Insanity is in Society.
Insanity is in Religion.
Insanity is in Politics.
Insanity is in Science.
Insanity is in Philosophy.
Insanity is in History.
Insanity is in Art.
Insanity is in Movies.
Insanity is in Television.
Insanity is in Entertainment.
Insanity is in Rituals.
Insanity is in Culture.
Insanity is in Schools.
Insanity is in Education.
Insanity is in "The System".
Insanity is in "The Establishment".
Insanity is in Money.
Insanity is in Capitalism.
Insanity is in Communism.
Insanity is in Fascism.
Insanity is in Militarism.

Insanity is in Monopolies.
Insanity is in Totalitarianism.
Insanity is in Dictatorships.
Insanity is in Nihilism.
Insanity is in Consumerism.
Insanity is in Conservativism.
Insanity is in Democracy.
Insanity is in Freedom.
Insanity is in Friendships.
Insanity is in Relationships.
Insanity is in Life.

Insanity is in Lo♥e.
Insanity is in Death.
Insanity is in Sin.
Insanity is in Sex.
Insanity is in Fucking.
Insanity is in not Fucking.
Insanity is in Heaven.
Insanity is in Hell.
Insanity is in Self.
Insanity is in Identity.
Insanity is in Possessiveness.
Insanity is in Humanity.

Insanity is Entertaining.
Insanity is Funny.
Insanity is Hilarious.
Insanity is Insane.
Insanity is GOOD!

"The Don"
25.08.2020

Lay with Me
(Sdraiti con Me)

Come over into my bed.
Come over & sleep with me.
Come over & let's conoodle.
Come over & let's spoon.
Come over & let's hold each other.
Come over & let's hug each other.
Come over & let's feel each other.
Come over & let's touch each other.
Come over & let's kiss each other.
Come over & let's lick each other.
Come over & let's taste each other.
Come over & let's smell each other.
Come over & let's rock each other.
Come over & let's fondle each other.
Come over & let's entwine in each other.
Come over & let's probe each other.
Come over & let's finger each other.
Come over & let's enter each other.
Come over & let's penetrate each.
Come over & let's fuck each other.
Come over & let's cum with each other.
Come over & let's get high with each other.
Come over & let's lie with each other.
Come over & let's sleep with each other.
Come over & let's Lo♥e each other.

"The Don"
24.08.2020

I Will Listen

(Ascolterò)

Got something on your mind?
I will listen.
Got something to say?
I will listen.
Got something to talk about?
I will listen.
Got something on your chest?
I will listen.
Got something you're worried about?
I will listen.
Got problems on your mind?
I will listen.
Got issues your concerned about?
I will listen.
Got relationship issues?
I will listen.
Got emotional issues?
I will listen.
Got sex issues?
I will listen.
Got Lo♥e issues?
I will listen.
Got problems with your best friend?
I will listen.
Got problems at work?
I will listen.
Got something you wanna say?
I will listen.
Got "*Existential*" concerns?
I will listen.
Got worries with the state of the Planet?
I will listen.
Got worries with the state of Politics?
I will listen.
Got issues with the Government?
I will listen.

Got issues with Society?
I will listen.
Got issues with Capitalism?
I will listen.
Got issues your Consumerism?
I will listen.
Got problems with being treated like an "*Object*"?
I will listen.
Got problems with being "*Dehumanised*"?
I will listen.
Got problems with "*Living*"?
I will listen.
Got problems with "*Dying*"?
I will listen.
Got problems with losing your "*Youth*"?
I will listen.
Got problems with getting "*Old*"?
I will listen.
Got issues with "*DEATH*"?
I will listen.
Got problems with "*Religion*"?
I will listen.
Got problems with "*Heaven*"?
I will listen.
Got problems going to "*HELL*"?
I will listen.
Got problems?
I will listen.
Got anything at all you wanna talk about?
I will listen.
I will listen.
I will listen.
I will listen.

"The Don"
25.08.2020

Yowie Woman

If you ever go to *"Far North Queensland"*?
If you ever go to *"Cape York Peninsula"*?
If you ever have the courage to go to *"The Great North Land"*?
You'll be in the *"Yidinji Nation"*.
Home of "Oka, The Black Queen of Glebe".

She tells me many stories.
Stories about her land in the *"Far North"*.
Stories that are *"Spiritual"*.
Stories that are about the *"Sacred Land"*.
Of the "Yowie Woman".
Mother of the "Land".

In the deep forest of *"Far North Queensland"*.
There spirits that roam the land.
That are with us.
In the day & in the night.
Sometimes, when it's quiet.
& there's no else about.
They'll appear to you.
They'll manifest their great light.
It could be the "Yowie Woman".
Mother of the "Land".

She might appear to if you're lucky.
If you are pure of heart & mind.
If you are deserving.
If your *"Soul"* is right.
If you are caring & kind.
The "Yowie Woman" might appear.
Mother of the "Land".

Her beauty is blinding.
Her radiance so bright.
Her smile is like the "Crescent Moon".
It lights up the night.
She is "Protector of the Earth".
Come to her blessings.
She shows herself to embrace you in her arms.
To envelope you in her warmth.
She is the "Yowie Woman".
Mother of the "Land".

She is the first "Woman".
She is the first "Wife".
She is the first "Mother".
She is the first "Bearer of Children".
She is the first "Nurture".
She is the first "Healer".
She is the first "Warrior".
She is the "Yowie Woman".
Mother of the "Land".

She provides energy to this sick planet.
That "White Men" are killing.
She provides strength to the "Black People" to keep struggling for their land.
She provides hope to the "Indigenous First Nation Peoples" that one day things will be made right.
She provides encouragement to "The White Men", to set things straight.
To say "We're Sorry".
To sign a "Treaty" in the Constitution.
To give the "Land" back.
She is the "Yowie Woman".
Mother of the "Land".

So, if you ever go to "Far North Queensland".
You'll be in the land of the "Yowie Woman".
Mother of the "Land".

(Inspired by "Oka, The Black Queen of Glebe)

"The Don"
26.08.2020

"Yowie Woman"
"Oka, The Black Queen of Glebe"

She's the Girl from Rio, Rio de Janerio

(Ela é a Menina de Rio, Rio de Janerio)

She came here for a holiday.
She didn't come to stay.
Now she can't go away.
She's the girl from Rio, Rio de Janerio.

She's homesick.
She wants to be back in Rio.
She wants to be with her friends.
She's the girl from Rio, Rio de Janerio.

She misses Cobacabana.
She misses Ibanema.
She misses the Salsa
She's the girl from Rio, Rio de Janerio.

She misses the fun.
She misses the nightlife.
She misses the People.
She's the girl from Rio, Rio de Janerio.

She has found a Lo♥e here.
She claims the sex is "GREAT".
She claims he's a "Nerdy Intellectual".
She's the girl from Rio, Rio de Janerio.

She just wants to have FUN.
She just wants to have a "good time".
She just to be back where she belongs.
She's the girl from Rio, Rio de Janerio.

She tries her BEST.
She tries so very hard.
But, Sydney ain't no Rio.
She's the girl from Rio, Rio de Janerio.

In her head she's back there.
In her head she's dancing the night away.
In her head she's on the beach in Cobacabanc.
She's the girl from Rio, Rio de Janerio.

She's dying inside.
She's lonely inside.
She's crying inside
She's the girl from Rio, Rio de Janerio.

One day she'll be back to Rio.
One day she will return to Rio.
One day she will live again in Rio.
She's the girl from Rio, Rio de Janerio.

"When my baby
When my baby smiles at me I go to Rio
De Janeiro, my-oh-me-oh
I go wild and then I have to do the Samba
And La Bamba
Now I'm not the kind of person
With a passionate persuasion for dancin'
Or roma-ancin'
But I give in to the rhythm
And my feet follow the beatin' of my hear-eart

Woh-ho-oh-oh, when my baby
When my baby smiles at me I go to Rio
De Janeiro
I'm a Salsa fellow
When my baby smiles at me
The sun'll lightens up my li-ife
And I am free at last, what a blast

Woh-ho-oh-oh, when my baby
When my baby smiles at me
I feel like Tarzan, of the Jungle
There on the hot sand
And in a bungalow while monkeys play above-a
We-ee make love-a
Now I'm not the type to let vibrations (Rio)
Trigger my imagination easily (Rio)
You know that's just not me
But I turn into a tiger (Rio)
Everytime I get beside the - one I love (Rio)
Woh, oh, woh, woh-oh, Rio - Rio
Yeah Ugh - Rio - Ugh

Woh-ho-oh-oh, when my ba-a-aby (when my baby)
When my baby smiles at me I go to Rio (Rio)
De Janeiro
I'm a Salsa fellow-ow
When my baby smiles at me
The sun'll lightens you-up my li-ife
And I am free at last, what a blast

When my baby (when my baby)
When my baby smiles at me I go to Rio (Rio)
That's when I go to Rio (Rio)
Rio - Rio De Janeir-eiro
Rio, Rio, Rio."

"I Go to Rio" Songwriters: Peter Allen/Adrienne Anderson

"The Don"
27.08.2020

"The girl from Rio, Rio de Janerio"

Money

Money IS the THING.
Money is the ONLY thing.
Money is the BIGGEST thing.
Money is the Issue.
Money is on everybody's lips.
Money is on everybody's Mind.
Money is in everybody's He♥rt.
Money is in everybody's Soul.
Money is in everybody's Being.

Everybody thinks about Money.
Everybody dreams about Money.
Everybody wants Money.
Everybody needs Money.
Everybody craves Money.
Everybody prostitutes for Money.

Money buys Riches.
Money buys Prestige.
Money buys Sex.
Money buys Power.
Money buys EVERYTHING.

Money can't buy Respect.
Money can't buy Compassion.
Money can't buy Friendship.
Money can't buy Kindness.
Money can't buy Caring.
Money can't buy Contentment.
Money can't buy "Peace of Mind".
Money can't buy Happiness.
Money can't buy Lo♥e.
Money can't buy Freedom.
Money can't buy Immortality.
Money can't buy ME.

Money doesn't shout, it SCREAMS!

"The best things in life are free
But you can keep them for the birds and bees
Now give me money
(That's what I want)
That's what I want
(That's what I want)
That's what I want, yeah (that's what I want)
That's what I want

Your lovin' gives me a thrill
But your lovin' don't pay my bills
Now give me money
(That's what I want)
That's what I want
(That's what I want)
That's what I want, yeah (that's what I want)
That's what I want

Money don't get everything, it's true
What it don't get, I can't use
Now give me money
(That's what I want)
That's what I want
(That's what I want)
That's what I want, yeah (that's what I want)
That's what I want, whoa

Money don't get everything, it's true
What it don't get, I can't use
Now give me money
(That's what I want)
That's what I want
(That's what I want)
That's what I want, yeah (that's what I want)
That's what I want

Well, now give me money
(That's what I want)
A lot of money
(That's what I want)
Wow, yeah, I wanna be free
(That's what I want)
A lot of money
That's what I want
That's what I want, well
(That's what I want)
Well, now give me money
(That's what I want)
A lot of money
(That's what I want)
Wow, yeah, you need money
(That's what I want)
Now, give me money
(That's what I want)
That's what I want, yeah (that's what I want)
That's what I want."

"Money" Songwriters: Janie Bradford/Berry Gordy Jr./Berry Jr Gordy

"The Don"
27.08.2020

Queen Sheila

She's an Amazonian Warrior.
She's a Viking Queen.
She's Mother Earth.
She's a traveller on this planet.
She's an Adventurer by birth.
She's courageous & strong.
She's fearless & fearsome.
She's hard as a rock.
She's as soft a cotton wool.
She's as old as the mountains.
She's as young as a new born babe.
She's as beautiful as the stars in the sky.
She's as intelligent as a library.
She's an adventurous adventurer.
She's on the journey, the journey called "Life".

I met her in 2019.
On the 1st of April.
April Fool's Day.
But it was no "April Fool's Joke" that day.
It was no joke at all.
She was dressed in purple.
The colour she always likes to wear.
She was sitting with her knees to her chin.
I guess it's for protection.
To say, "keep away"!
Vaping away, as she liked to do.
I was taken straight away.
Swept away by her profile.
Her perfectly formed shaven head.
Like a smoothly polished gemstone.

I introduced myself.
I asked her if I could sit down beside her.
I asked her if I could feel her scalp.
She looked at me with a quizzical gaze.
As though she was thinking, "What sort of request is that?"
To my amazement she said yes.
I was a little bit shocked that she agreed.
But, also very excited.
I gently ran my right hand over her recently shaved head.
I could feel the bristles of her new grown hair.
I felt the perfectly rounded form of her skull.
Her narrow nape of her neck.
I knew then that she was someone "Special".

She's had many adventures since that day.
I don't see anymore.
Maybe we'll meet again someday?
Maybe our paths will cross again?
Maybe I'll get to feel her head again?
Maybe she'll tell me of all her new adventures?
Maybe, I'll be a better listener this time?
Maybe?

"The Don"
29.08.2020

Laughter is the Name of the Game
(La Risata è il Nome del Gioco)

What game are you playing?
What are the boundaries?
Are you having FUN?
Are you enjoying it?
Is it bringing you Happiness?
Is it bringing you laughter?
Because laughter is the name of the game.

If there is no Humour?
If there is no Fun?
If there is no Frivolity?
If there is no laughter?
You are playing the wrong game.
Because laughter is the name of the game.

Life should be Fun.
Life should be Enjoyable.
Life should be Happy.
Life should be Rewarding.
If not, you are playing the wrong game.
Because laughter is the name of the game.

Life is a Game.
Life is a Sport.
Life is a Joke.
Life is not to be taken Seriously.
Life is for having Fun.
Life is for having a "Good Time".
Life is about laughter.
Life is a about have a "Sense of Humour".
Because laughter is the name of the game.

If there is no laughter in your life,
Or the laughter is gone.
You are playing the wrong game.
Because laughter is the name of the game.

"The Don"
29.08.2020

The Wonderful Land of Oz

We're off to discover the wonderful,
The wonderful "Land of Oz"!
Why?
Because, because, because, because!
We're off to find the wonderful,
The wonderful "Land of Oz"!
Why?
Because, because, because, because!
We're off to see the wonderful,
The wonderful "Land of Oz"!
Why?
Because, because, because, because!
We're off to experience the wonderful,
The wonderful "Land of Oz"!
Why?
Because, because, because, because!
We're off to enjoy the wonderful,
The wonderful "Land of Oz"!
Why?
Because, because, because, because!
We're off to explore the wonderful,
The wonderful "Land of Oz"!
Why?
Because, because, because, because!
We're off to steal the wonderful,
The wonderful "Land of Oz"!
Why?
Because, because, because, because!
We're off to take over the wonderful,
The wonderful "Land of Oz"!
Why?
Because, because, because, because!
We're off to claim the wonderful,
The wonderful "Land of Oz"!
Why?
Because, because, because, because!
We're off to rename the wonderful,
The wonderful "Land of Oz"!
Why?
Because, because, because, because!
We're off to repopulate the wonderful,
The wonderful "Land of Oz"!
Why?
Because, because, because, because!
We're off to re-educate the wonderful,
The wonderful "Land of Oz"!
Why?
Because, because, because, because!
We're off to Spiritualise the wonderful,
The wonderful "Land of Oz"!
Why?
Because, because, because, because!

We're off to exploit the wonderful,
The wonderful "Land of Oz"!
Why?
Because, because, because, because!
We're off to consume the wonderful,
The wonderful "Land of Oz"!
Why?
Because, because, because, because!
We're off to devour the wonderful,
The wonderful "Land of Oz"!
Why?
Because, because, because, because!
We're off to mine the wonderful,
The wonderful "Land of Oz"!
Why?
Because, because, because, because!
We're off to burn the wonderful,
The wonderful "Land of Oz"!
Why?
Because, because, because, because!
We're off to destroy the wonderful,
The wonderful "Land of Oz"!
Why?
Because, because, because, because!
We're off to eradicate the wonderful,
The wonderful "Land of Oz"!
Why?
Because, because, because, because!
We're off to annihilate the wonderful,
The wonderful "Land of Oz"!
Why?
Because, because, because, because!
We're off to FUCK the wonderful,
The wonderful "Land of Oz"!
Why?
Because, because, because, because!
We're off to Dehumanise We're off to annihilate the wonderful,
The wonderful "Land of Oz"!
Why?
Because, because, because, because!
We're off to Fuck the wonderful,
The wonderful "Land of Oz"!
Why?
Because, because, because, because!
Why?
Because, because, because, because!

The wonderful,
The wonderful "Land of Oz"!

The wonderful,
The wonderful "Land of Oz"!

"The Don"
29.08.2020

Night Time
(la Notte)

Night Time is the Dark time.
Night Time is the Moonlight time.
Night Time is the Lonely time.
Night Time is the Play time.
Night Time is the Scary time.
Night Time is the Demon time.
Night Time is the Witching time.
Night Time is the Ghost time.
Night Time is the Shadows time.
Night Time is the Howling time.
Night Time is the Shining time.
Night Time is the Terror time.
Night Time is the Revenge time.
Night Time is the Stalking time.
Night Time is the Killing time.
Night Time is the DEAD time.
Night Time is the HELL time.
Night Time is the Walking Dead time.
Night Time is the Zombie time.
Night Time is the FUCKING time.

I Lo♥e Night Time!

"The Don"
29.08.2020

I'm a Failure

(Sono un Fallimento)

I'm a failure.
That's what I am.

I'm a failure in my career.
I'm a failure in my Lo♥e.
I'm a failure in Life.

I don't know what I'm doing.
I don't know where I'm going.
I don't know what is happening.
I don't know anything.

I must be delusional.
I must be crazy.
I must be insane.
I'm a failure.

I don't know what's going on.
I don't know what's going down.
I don't know the rules.
I don't know how to play the game.
I'm a failure.

Please, set me straight.
Please, set me right.
Please, show me how it's done.
I'm a failure in Life.

I think I know what's going on.
I think I know the score.
I think I've got it together.
I think I'm doing ok.
I think I'm on top.
I think I'm gonna score.
I'm a failure.

I think I'm a nice guy.
I think I'm interesting.
I think I'm intelligent.
I think I'm Cool.
I think I'm Sexy.
I think I'm passionate.
I think I'm sensual.
I think I'm a Lo♥er.
I'm just a failure.

I think I'm Kind.
I think I'm Caring.
I think I'm Respectful.
I think I'm Compassionate.
I think I'm Friendly.

I'm just a failure.

I'm a Failure

"The Don"
29.08.2020

Lo♥e Sick
(Amore Malato)

It's FIRE in your belly.
It's churning & burning.
It's turning you inside out.
You can't control it.
It messes with your stomach.
It messes with your Mind.
It messes with your He♥rt.
It messes with your Blood.
You've got it BAD.
You're Lo♥e Sick.

You try to fight it.
You try to bring it under control.
You try to be its Master.
But it just won't let go.
It's a got a hold of you "real" good.
You just have to admit.
That you're Lo♥e Sick.

It's a constant struggle.
You think you're on top of it.
But it comes back again.
It's a very tough opponent.
It keeps fighting till the End.
Do have the energy to keep on getting?
Do you have the strength to fight till End?
Or will you throw in the towel?
Admit defeat & succumb to its will.
Bow down to its power.
It's mastery over you.
Accept that you are just a "weakling".
That are in its grip.
You are Lo♥e Sick.

But what are the symptoms?
How will you know you've got it?
Through "Self-diagnosis".
Ask yourself these simple questions.
And you will immediately be able to tell.

Do you wanna own them?
Do you want them in your pocket?
Do you want them at your "beck & call"?
Do you wanna know their every move?
Where they're been?
Who they're with?
Who they're seeing?
Who they're fucking?

If you answer "Yes" to these questions.
You've got it "real" bad.
You'll have to take some medicine.
Because, you are Lo❤e Sick.

You have caught the sickness.
You have caught the disease.
Is a bacteria or is it a virus?
Or maybe, none of these?
Science has no cure.
There are no antibiotics that be prescribed.
There is no vaccine that you can take.
There is nothing you can do?
You just gotta to ride it out.
Maybe, take some drugs to numb your mind.
Like alcohol or marijuana.
Or maybe go "Cold Turkey".
Until it's gone through you.
That's about all you can do.
When you are Lo❤e Sick.

"I'm walking through streets that are dead
Walking, walking with you in my head
My feet are so tired, my brain is so wired
And the clouds are weeping

Did I hear someone tell a lie?
Did I hear someone's distant cry?
You thrilled me to my heart, then you ripped it all apart
You went through my pockets when I was sleeping

I'm sick of love...but I'm in the thick of it
This kind of love...I'm so sick of it

I see lovers in the meadow
I see silhouettes in the window
I watch them 'til they're gone and they leave me hanging on
To a shadow

I'm sick of love...I hear the clock tick
This kind of love...I'm love sick

Sometimes the silence can be like the thunder
Sometimes I feel like I'm being plowed under
Could you ever be true? I think of you
And I wonder

I'm sick of love...I wish I'd never met you
I'm sick of love...I'm trying to forget you

Just don't know what to do
I'd give anything to be with you"

"Love Sick" Songwriter: Bob Dylan

"The Don"
30.08.2020

Karma

Do you believe in Karma?
Do you believe in Fate?
Do you believe in Destiny?

Karma is a BITCH!
It'll come & bite you in the bum.
What will be will be.
What goes round comes round.

Your actions come back.
They always do.
When you least expect it.
They will slap you in the face.

Come back to Reality.
Don't live in a Dream.
Don't live a life of delusion.
Open your eyes & see.

You are what you do!
You receive what you give.
No more, no less.
This is the equation.

It's very simple indeed.
Nothing more complicated than that.
It's not a mysterious Black Hole.
It's a fact & that's that.

Give Uncaring, receive Uncaring.
Give Disrespect, receive Disrespect.
Give Anger, receive Anger.
Give Jealousy, receive Jealousy.
Give Hate, receive Hate.

Give Kindness, receive Kindness.
Give Respect, receive Respect.
Give Compassion, receive Compassion.
Give Friendship, receive Friendship.
Give Love, receive Love.

That's it.
That's how Karma works.
No more than that.
There are no magic tricks.
No mysterious incantations.

Karma is Universal.
Karma is Irreversible.
Karma is Unpredictable.
Karma is Destiny.

Karma is a BITCH!

"The Don"
31.08.2020

Why Do You Have to Make Relationships Work?

(Perché Devi Far Funzionare le Relazioni?)

Why do you have to make relationships work?
Shouldn't they be easy?
Natural?
Organic?
Fluidic?

Why do you have to make relationships work?
Why do you have to "MAKE" them work?
Why do you have to "FORCE" them to work?
And what does "WORK" mean anyway?
To stay with a person out of,
Compromise?
Obligation?
Commitment?
Even though they treated you badly?

Why do you have to make relationships work?
Why do you have to "MAKE" them work?
Stay because of the children?
The pets?
The house?
The image?
The prestige?
The religion?
The family?

Why do you have to make relationships work?
If the Lo♥e is gone?
If there is no Respect?
If there is no Kindness?
If there is no Caring?
If there is no Compassion?
If there is no Friendship?

Why do you have to make relationships work?
Why struggle?
Why suffer?
Why cry?
Why agonise?
Why stay?
Why?

Why do you have to make relationships work?
If it's broken?
Why should you fix it?
Why not just move on?
Establish new friendships?
Establish new relationships?
Experience new Lo♥e?

Why do you have to make relationships work?
Is it fear?
Is it lack of self-belief?
Is it poor self-image?
Is it lack of confidence?
Is it a "delusional" idea of Lo♥e?
Is it an "Idealised" idea of Lo♥e?
Is it Religious beliefs?
Is it just comfortable?
Is it "Better the Devil you know"?
Is it "Out of the frying pan & into the fire"?

Why do you have to make relationships work?

Because someone said so!

"The Don"
31.08.2020

If You Can't Play with Somebody Else, Play with Yourself!

(Se Non Puoi Giocare con Qualcun Altro, Gioca con te Stesso!)

If you're *all alone*.
If you're *by yourself*.
If you're *feeling down*.
If you're *feeling pained*.
If you're *suffering, from unrequited Lo♥e*.
If you can't play with the one you Lo♥e.
Play with yourself.

If you Lo♥er has *let you down*.
If you Lo♥er has *busted your crown*.
If you Lo♥er has *thrown away the key*.
If you Lo♥er has *put you out to sea*.
If you can't play with the one you Lo♥e.
Play with yourself.

If you're stuck *in your room*.
If you're stuck *by yourself*.
If you're stuck *all alone*.
If you're stuck all *by yourself*.
If you can't play with the one you Lo♥e.
Play with yourself.

I know it's *second best*.
I know it's *not what you'd like*.
I know it's *not what you'd want*.
I know it's *all you're gonna get*.
'Cause, if you can't play with the one you Lo♥e.
Play with yourself.

"The Don"
31.08.2020

The Muse

Let *The Muse* take you.
Make sure to write it down.
Let it take control.
Don't stop the flow.
Let it flow freely.
Just let it go.
Let *The Muse* take you.
Wherever it wants to go.

It knows what it doing.
The Muse knows the way.
It been there many times before.
As long as you let it have its way.
Don't stop.
Don't try to control it.
Don't overthink it.
Just let *The Muse* go.

It knows what to say.
It's said all before.
Nobody ever listens though.
Everybody thinks they know the score.
The story's as old as the mountains.
Maybe even older.
It's been told a million times.
And it'll be told a million more.
But it worth repeating.
It's worth to hear it again.
Every time I hear it.
It's as though I've never heard it before.
It's as if I'm hearing it for the very first time.

The Muse is a very good storyteller.
It knows how to spin a yarn.
It'll be about lost Lo♥e.
About how your He♥rt was broken.
By the "*Girl from the Red River Shore*".
Don't shed any tears.
Now's not the time to cry.
The Muse has got you.

You cannot let it die.
It won't let you.
You are powerless in its hands.
Give yourself to *The Muse*.
Fulfill its every demand.

The Muse is a Spiritual entity.
It knows what it wants.
You must let it consume you completely.
You must not but up a fight.
Do you trust it?
Will you let it have control?
Will you let it do what it's come to do?
Will you carry out its mission?

There is nothing to fear.
Except of course, fear itself.
This is the only thing that can stop it.
Stop it in its tracks.
Yes, there could be "*Blood on the tracks*".
There could be "*Blood on the carpet*".
It would be an awful sight.
The battle of the century.
The Muse will put up a good fight.

It won't die without giving it it's all.
It definitely won't throw in the towel.
No never, not at all.
It will fight till the bitter end.
Until every last drop of blood has been shed.
Even then it will still keep fighting.
Because it knows it's worth fighting for.

When the smoke has finally cleared.
When the battle has been lost & won.
The Muse will stand triumphantly.
Albeit, bloodied & bruised.
Its story has been told.
Its song has been sung.
The sun is rising.
The Muse has won.

The Muse may return someday, maybe?

"The Don"
01.09.2020

I Must've Done Something Wrong

(Devo aver Fatto Qualcosa di Sbagliato)

I must've said the wrong thing.
I must've spoke out of turn.
I must've upset her somehow.
I must've opened my big, fat mouth.
I must've put my foot into it.
I must've sat in the wrong chair.
I must've done it this time.
I must've made the wrong move.
I must've said the wrong words.
I must've sung the wrong song.
I must've played in the wrong key.
I must've played the wrong instrument.
I must've told the wrong joke.
I must've talked out of turn.
I must've touched her in the wrong place.
I must've touched her there.
I must've stroked hair in the wrong place.
I must've drunk her beer.
I must've licked the wrong ear.
I must've kissed the wrong lips.
I must've felt the wrong feelings.
I must've read the wrong signs.
I must've gone down the wrong road.
I must've taken the wrong path.
I must've made the wrong turn.
I must've turned right instead of turning left.
I must've gone straight ahead.
I must've not stopped for a break.
I must've not seen the signs.
I must've been blinded by the lights.
I must've been too stupid not to see it coming.
I must've been outta my mind.
Are you pissed off with me?
She's not calling back.

"The Don"
01.09.2020

Yes

(Si)

Always say "Yes".
It's a great way to go.
It'll take you to places I.
You've never been before.

Yes, to a good time.
Yes, to adventure.
Yes, to for more.
Yes, to all that & much, much more.

Yes, you won't know where it'll take you.
Yes, it's a little bit risky.
Yes, it's a little bit scary.

Yes, let's open the door.
Yes, let's go crazy.
Yes, let's let it all go.
Yes, let's say "Why not?"
Yes, let's give it a shot.
Yes, let's try something new.
Yes, let's try something different.
Yes, let's break those chains that bind us.
Yes, let's give it a whirl.
Yes, let's give it a try.
Yes, let's fly really high.
Yes, let's get "stoned" out of our heads.
Yes, let's stay all day in bed.
Yes, let's fuck all night long.
Yes, let's sing that beautiful song.
Yes, let's drink that "Pina Colada".
Yes, let's swim naked in the ocean.
Yes, let's go to Copacabana.
Yes, let's go to Rio.

Yes, let's make Lo♥e in the rain.
Yes, let's do it again & again.
Yes, let's dance in the Streets.
Yes, let's have gelato at the "Trevi Fountain".
Yes, let's go to Paris.
Yes, let's go tell Edith Piaf that we have "No regrets".
Yes, let's go say "Hello, I Lo♥e you".
Yes, let's go visit "Jim Morrison's" grave at Pere Lachaise Cemetery.
Yes, let's see the Aurora Borealis.
Yes, let's stay in the "Ice Palace".
Yes, let's go to Petra.
Yes, let's visit where it all began.
Yes, let's go to the birth of civilization.
Yes, let's go to "Far North Queensland".
Yes, let's go into the deep, dark forest.
Yes, let's try to see the "Yowie Man".
Yes, let's go to "Paradise Island".
Yes, let's take the "Stairway to Heaven".
Yes, let's drive on "Highway to Hell".
Yes, let's come back by "Highway 61".
Yes, let's stop & stay in "Hotel California".
Yes, let's take the soap & say "We made it out alive!"
Yes, let's go to the "Dead Heart".
Yes, let's go to the "Red Centre".
Yes, let's go visit the "Solid Rock".
Yes, let's pray at "Uluru".

Yes, let's enjoy this "one" Life.
Yes, let's make it a "great" Life.
Yes, let's have a "Wonderful" one.

Yes, what else you got to do?
Yes, why not?
Yes, "Can I come too?"
Yes, "Come on, let's go have some fun!"

"The Don"
01.09.2020

Abused

(Abusata)

You are used.
You are fused.
You are mused.
You are bemused.
You are amused.
You are unamused.
You are confused.
You are infused.
You are refused.
You are suffused.
You are diffused.
You are redused.
You are prodused.
You are reused.
You are excused.
You are unexcused.
You are transfused.
You are perused.
You are disused.
You are pre-used.
You are underused.
You are overused.
You are accused.
You are A & b used.
You are Abused.

Don't be ABUSED!

"The Don"
02.09.2020

Your Eyes

(I tuoi Occhi)

Don't speak using word.
Don't speak using your mouth.
You don't have to say a thing.
You don't have to use your lips.
Speak with your Eyes.
They say everything.
They can talk vast amounts.
Just with one look.

They say that "*Your eyes are the portals into your Soul*".
Well, if this is true you are immense as the Universe.
The language they speak everyone can understand.
You don't need an interpreter to tell you what they say.
One bat of an eyelid.
One spark of light.
One soft seductive look.
That's all I need to understand.

You don't have to speak.
Words are so clumsy & inadequate.
The Eyes speak so beautifully & eloquently.
So direct & so true.
One look is all I need.
To know what you say.
To understand what you want.
To say that you Lo❤e me.

Your Eyes are the conduit to my He❤rt.
They are so direct & immediate.
Like a bullet shot in the dark.
At the speed of light.
They can make me or break me.
Shoot me into the Heavens.
Or make me fall into the depths of Hell.
With a look of your Eyes.
I can see everything.
What has been, what is & what will be.
With one look of your Eyes I know where I stand.
If there is going to be a tonight?
If there will be a tomorrow?

The Eyes say it all.
The Eyes are the pathway into your & my very Soul.

"The Don"
02.09.2020

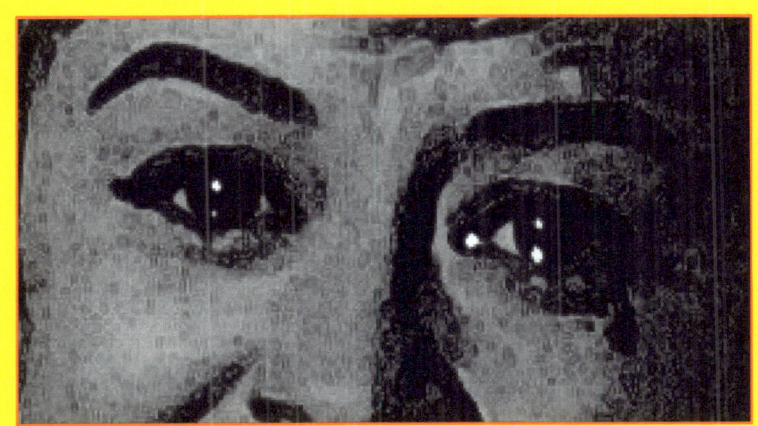

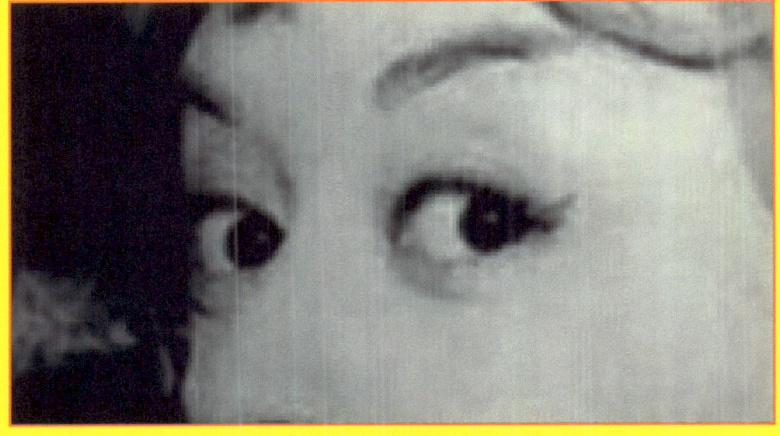

Giuletta Masina

Unrequited Love
(Amore non Restituito)

The Heart wants what it wants.
The Heart sees what it sees.
The Heart hears what it hears.
The Heart feels what it feels.
The Heart thinks what it thinks.
The Heart needs what it needs.
The Heart desires what it desires.
The Heart chases what it chases.
The Heart pursues what it pursues.
The Heart believes what it believes.
The Heart longs for what it longs.
The Heart possesses what it possesses.
The Heart screams for what it screams.
The Heart yearns for what it yearns.
The Heart dreams for what it dreams.
The Heart cries for what it cries.
The Heart suffers for what it suffers.
The Heart pains for what it pains.
The Heart explodes for what it explodes.
The Heart breaks for what it breaks.

The Heart has a Mind of its own.
The Heart cannot be controlled.
The Heart is what it is.
The Heart is The Heart.

"The Don"
03.09.2020

I Woke Up with a Hard On
(Mi Sono Svegliato con Un'erezione)

What does this mean?
What is it all about?
Is this a sign of what to come?
I woke up with a hard on.

Did I have sexy dreams?
Of unfulfilled desires?
Did I have wet dreams?
Of fulfilled passions?
'Cause, I woke up with a hard on.

Could it mean a good day?
Could it mean I will get "lucky"?
Maybe, tonight is the night?
Maybe, tonight I fulfil my dreams.
'Cause, I woke up with a hard on.

I don't want to go home with a hard on.
Remember what Leonard Cohen said.
"It'll only drive you insane!"
So, don't go home with a hard on.
Especially when I woke up with a hard on.

I'll take it a positive.
I'll take as a good omen.
I'll take it as sign from God.
'Cause, I woke up with a hard on.

"The Don"
04.09.2020

I Give Up

What's the point?
That's it.
It's fucking a waste of time.
You just get knocked over.
How many times can you keep getting back up?
Only to get knocked back down again.
I give up.

You try your best.
You give it your all.
You think you've done all you can do.
But it's still not enough.
You're still not good enough.
I give up.

Sooner or later you've got to admit defeat.
Sooner or later you've got to say enough.
Sooner or later you've gotta throw in the towel.
Sooner or later you gotta call it quits.
Sooner or later you gotta give up.
So, I give up.

There is no point in going on.
There is no point in being rejected again.
The outcome is so obviously predictable.
You don't need to suffer it again.
Just give up & walk away.

You are weak & pathetic.
You fall into the same old trap.
You never learn from your mistakes.
You just keep repeating them over & over again.
You gotta give up.

Take tonight for instance.
Did you have to text?
You knew what her response would be.
But you did it anyway.
You could see it coming from a mile away.
But you just couldn't help yourself?
You did it anyway.
Just give up.

You know what the situation is.
You don't need to be told.
She is telling you anyway.
Silence is a word.
Her silence is talking to you.
You know what she is saying.
"Don't ring me, I'll ring you!"
So, give up.

If she wanted to see you, she would ring you.
That the message.
It's plainly crystal clear.
Accept this & move on.
Don't linger & hang on.
Cut the chain & let her go.
Resign yourself to this fact.
And say, I give up!

I Give Up

"The Don"
04.09.2020

Your Tribe

Have you found your *Friends*?
Have you found your *People*?
Have you found your *Nation*?
Have you found your *Country*?
Have you found your *Land*?
Have you found your *World*?
Have you found your *Planet*?
Have you found your *Universe*?
Have you found your *Home*?
Have you found your *Place*?
Have you found your *Lo♥es*?
Have you found your *Family*?
Have you found *Your Tribe*?

Have you found where you *belong*?
Have you found where you supposed to *be*?
Have you found where you are *happy*?
Have you found where you don't have to *pretend*?
Have you found where you can be *yourself*?
Have you found where you are accepted for who you *are*?
Have you found where you can be free to *be*?
Have you found where you are among your *people*?
Have you found where you are Lo♥ed for who you *are*?
Have you found where you are with *friends*?
Have you found *Your Tribe*?

Your tribe gives you *Strength*.
Your tribe gives you *Support*.
Your tribe gives you *Security*.
Your tribe gives you *Nourishment*.
Your tribe gives you *Energy*.
Your tribe gives you *Respect.*
Your tribe gives you *Kindness*.
Your tribe gives you *Friendship*.
Your tribe gives you *Nurturing*.
Your tribe gives you *Lo♥e*.
Your tribe gives you *Family*.
Have you found *Your Tribe*?

"The Don"
05.09.2020

It is What it is

(È Quello Che è)

It will be what it will be.
There's no point making a fuss about it.
There's no point jumping up & down.
There's nothing you can do at it.
There's nothing you can say.
Just accept it & move on.
There's always another day.
There's always a new morning.
There's always a new start.
Just learn from your Past.
And don't repeat your mistakes.
Although, that is easier said than done.
Especially if you have a "Hard head" like me.
"Testa dura!"
I NEVER learn.
I always think, "Give it one more try!"
That's "one" try to many.
I should've stopped before.
But "Oh no"!
I had to give it one more go.
So, I'm an Idiot.
What can I do?
Just learn to accept things as they.
And not force them to the End.
To accept it & say "It is what it is".

"The Don"
05.09.2020

Do Not Think

(Non Pensare)

Do not speak.
Do not talk.
Do not plan.
Do not expect.
Do not anticipate.
Do not possess.
Do not attach.
Do not own.
Do not control.
Do not seek.
Do not pursue.
Do not stalk.
Do not fantasise.
Do not imagine.
Do not dream.
Do not theorise.
Do not hypothesise.
Do not postulate.
Do not formulate.
Do not emotionalise.
Do not dramatise.
Do not formulise.
Do not rationalise.
Do not suffocate.
Do not concentrate.
Do not THINK!

"The Don"
05.09.2020

You need Love

(Hai Bisogno di Amore)

You need protection.
You need shelter.
You need being taken care of.
You need Love.

You need reassurance.
You need attention.
You need kindness.
You need Love.

You need to be held.
You need to be hugged.
You need to be rocked.
You need Love.

You need security.
You need gentleness.
You need softness.
You need Love.

You are a child inside.
You've had a tough life.
You've done a lot in your live.
You need Love.

You've been married twice.
You've had a powerful job.
You've travelled the World.
You need Love.

You've been hurt.
You've been abused.
You've been let down.
You need Love.

You have insecurities.
You have doubts.
You have fears.
You need Lo♥e.

You've been hurt.
You've been rejected.
You've been abandoned.
You need Lo♥e.

You are tough.
You are strong.
You are independent.
You need Lo♥e.

You are fucking bitch.
You are fearless.
You are a warrior.
You need Lo♥e.

You say "the World is shit".
You say "people are bad".
You say "you don't need anyone".
But you need Lo♥e.

I can see it in your Eyes.
I can see it in your He♥rt.
I can see it in your Soul!
You need Lo♥e.

We all need Lo♥e.
That's nothing to be ashamed of.
We all need to be Lo♥ed.
You need Lo♥e.

"The Don"
06.09.2020

The Girl with the Large Labia Lips
(La Ragazza con le Grandi Labia Labbra)

"I have large labia lips".
That's what she said to me.
"Do you know what I mean?"
She asked.
"Of course!", I replied.
"Well, I can't verify that because I've never seen them", I said.
"Show me & I'll tell you if it's true".
"Purely from a Scientific point of view", I told her.
"Have you seen a lot of labia lips?", she asked.
"I've seen a few", I answered.
"Not millions, though".
"But I've seen my fair share in porn".
"So, I should be okay".
"To tell you, if you're The Girl with the Large Labia Lips".

She's "The Girl from Ipanema".
She's "The Girl from Copacabana".
She's "The Girl from Rio".
She's "The Girl from Brazil".
She's "The Girl from Tokyo".
She's "The Girl from New York City".
She's "The Girl from the North Country".
She's "The Girl with Spider Tattoo".
She's "The Girl with the Golden Hair".
She's "The Girl who Just Wants to have Fun".
She's "The Girl with the Large Labia Lips".

She's "The China Girl".
She's "The Uptown Girl".
She's "The Brown Eyed Girl".
She's "The Material Girl".
She's "The Girl on Film".
She's "The Rich Girl".
She's "The Cinnamon Girl".
She's "The Barbie Girl".
She's "The Island Girl".
She's "The Beach Girl".
She's "The Candy Girl".
She's "The Bad Girl".
She's "The Dirty Little Girl".
She's "The Fucking Bitch Girl"
She's "The Girl with the Large Labia Lips".

"The Don"
07.09.2020

You Got Something to Say?

(Hai Qualcosa da Dire?)

You got something to say?
Tell me about it.
You got something to say?
Speak your mind.
You got something to say?
Don't hold back.
You got something to say?
Let me have it.
You got something to say?
Whatever it is.
You got something to say?
I can handle it.
You got something to say?
Don't be shy.
You got something to say?
Get it off your chest.
You got something to say?
Don't leave anything out.
You got something to say?
Start from the beginning.
You got something to say?
I'm not going anywhere.
You got something to say?
I've got nowhere to go.
You got something to say?
Take your time.
You got something to say?
Collect your thoughts.
You got something to say?
You don't need to rush.
You got something to say?
I'm not going anywhere.
You got something to say?
You can shout if you like.
You got something to say?
You can say whatever you like.
You got something to say?
Don't censor yourself.

You got something to say?
You can swear if you like.
You got something to say?
I won't object.
You got something to say?
I won't put up a fight.
You got something to say?
I won't argue back.
You got something to say?
You can call me a "motherfucker".
You got something to say?
If you like?
You got something to say?
Go straight for the jugular.
You got something to say?
Why not?
You got something to say?
Make it as good as you can.
You got something to say?
Take this opportunity.
You got something to say?
It may never come again.
You got something to say?
Just let me have it.
You got something to say?
Don't hold back.
You got something to say?
Wait, let me sit down.
You got something to say?
Okay, go for it.
You got something to say?
Now's your chance.
You got something to say?
Don't blow it though?
You got something to say?
Who knows what the Future will bring?
You got something to say?
Speak now or forever hold your tongue.
You got something to say?

"The Don"
08.09.2020

The Witching Hour

(L'ora delle Streghe)

It's that time of the morning.
Between night time & daylight.
When the Spirits return to their graves.
When the ghosts disappear.
When the Cock sings his song.
It's *The Witching Hour*.

Don't go out.
Stay in bed.
Don't get caught in the rush.
The vampires are having their last drink.
The day is coming.
No time to waste.
They can't get caught.
It's *The Witching Hour*.

The Spirit World is returning home.
They have worked all night long.
Their work is finished.
They have done what they had to do.
Stay out of their way!
They can't get caught by the Daylight.
It's *The Witching Hour*.

They'll be back tomorrow tonight.
They'll make sure of that.
To take up where they left off.
To complete any unfinished business.
To start a new job.
But that'll have to wait.
Because now is *The Witching Hour*.

If you hear strange noises.
Stay safe in your bed.
But your head under the covers.
It's "*Twilight Time*".
It's "*The Crack of Dawn*".
Don't open your eyes.
Until *The Witching Hour* is over.

"The Don"
08.09.2020

She's in Control

(Ha il Controllo)

She decides what she wants.
She decides what she gets.
She decides what she needs.
She's in Control.

She decides when she wants it.
She decides where she wants it.
She decides with whom she wants it.
She's in Control.

She decides the time.
She decides the place.
She decides for how long.
She's in Control.

She has the Power.
She has the whip.
She has the last say.
She's in Control.

She's the Boss.
She's the Ruler.
She's the Queen.
She's in Control.

She makes the rules.
She makes the decisions.
She makes the plays.
She's in Control.

She's the referee.
She's the adjudicator.
She's the judge.
She's in Control.

"The Don"
08.09.2020

I'm in Deep

(Sono In Profondità)

I've fallen for you.
You've got me hooked.
I've taken the bait.
In fact, I've shallowed the hook too.
I'm in Deep.

I've been caught.
I've been snagged.
I've been snared.
I've been trapped.
I'm in Deep.

No use in struggling.
No use in trying to escape.
No use in trying to run.
No use in fighting it.
I'm in Deep.

Accept your situation.
Accept your predicament.
Accept your fate.
Accept your infatuation.
I'm in Deep.

Just go for the ride.
Follow the path.
Enjoy your journey.
There's no place to hide.
It's gonna be tough, maybe?
I'm in Deep.

"The Don"
09.09.2020

A CRY

(Un Piangere)

A cry in the *dark*.
A cry in the *night*.
A cry in the *daylight*.
A cry in the *wilderness*.
A cry in the *bushes*.
A cry in the *forest*.
A cry in the *desert*.

A *plaintive* cry.
A *he♥rt felt* cry.
A *broken he♥rted* cry.
A *distraught* cry.
A *mournful* cry.
A *painful* cry.
A *weeping* cry.
A *sorrowful* cry.
A *lonely* cry.
A *dreaded* cry.
A *Deathly* cry.
A *Deadly* cry.
A *blood curdling* cry.

A cry of *horror*.
A cry for *help*.
A cry from the *He♥rt*.
A cry from the *Soul*.
Cry me a river.
I cry.

"The Don"
09.09.2020

You're a Fascist!
(Sei un Fascista!)

Who do you think you are?
Telling me what to do.
You have the gall.
Thinking that you can dictate what I should do?
What I can & can't do?
You're a Fascist!

What an arsehole.
You're fucked in the head.
What's up your arse?
Dickhead!
I didn't realise you were such a "Control" freak!
You're a Fascist!

Man, I didn't realise what a prick you were.
As if I give a shit about you, anyway.
You don't even figure in my thoughts.
Let alone in "My World".
You're a Fascist!

It's no skin off my nose.
No burden on my back.
You mean nothing to me.
You don't even exist.
In fact, you have the personality of a "limp dick".
You're just a Fascist!

You wanna be the "Big Boss Man".
You want to control.
You want power.
You want to tell people what to do.
You're just a Fascist!

Stay in your cubby hole.
That's where you belong.
You only come out to spread you poison.
To spray your venom everywhere.
Anyway, I've blocked you on "insta", so there!
You're just a Fascist!

"The Don"
09.09.2020

Equilibrium

(Equilibrio)

A question of "Balance".
Being "Centred".
The "Ying & Yang".
Using "Feng Shui".
Letting it "Flow".
Have it "All Together".
Being "Equilibrated".
Being "Unified".
Being in "Internal Peace".
Having "Internal Peace".
Having "Self-Control".
Having no "Internal Conflict".
Having no "Internal Noise".
Being "Self-Aware".
"Self-Liberation".
Having "Self-Consciousness".
Being "Aware of your Actions".
A "Higher Level of Consciousness".
"Intentionality".
"Non-Mechanicity".
The "Mobius Loop".
Experiencing "The FORCE".

"The Don"
09.09.2020

I Am

(Io Sono)

I am a fake.
I am a fraud.
I am a hypocrite.
I am a shyster.
I am a manipulator.
I am a consumer.
I am a devourer.
I am a destroyer.
I am a fixer.
I am a movie star.
I am a nothing.
I am a nobody.
I am a no one.
I am a feeling.
I am a thought.
I am a theory.
I am a hypothesis.
I am a formula.
I am a logarithm.
I am a fallen star.
I am a supernova.
I am a pulsar.
I am a quasar.
I am a galaxy.
I am a black hole.
I am a quark.

I am a cock.
I am a chicken.
I am a duck.
I am a hero.
I am a coward.
I am a weakling.
I am a ghost.
I am a chameleon.
I am a changeling.
I am a vampire.
I am a dickhead.
I am a prick.
I am a parasite.
I am a virus.
I am a saint.
I am a sinner.
I am a hater.
I am a Lo♨er.
I am a saviour.
I am a Being.
I am a Soul.
I am a He♥rt.
I am a God.
I am a Devil.
I am a prayer.
I am a virgin.
I am a fertilised egg.
I am a Human Being.
I am a DELUSION.

"The Don"
10.09.2020

I'm Not Going to Sleep with You!
(Non Vado a Letto con Te)

Would you to stay the night?
Would you you like to sleep with me?
We don't have to fuck.
Not if you don't want to.
We can just hold each other right.
Hug each other through the night.
Although I will probably get a hard on.
Put don't worry about him.
It won't do anything.
Unless you want him to?
We can spoon each.
Cradle in each other's arms.
Naked flesh to naked flesh.
Just like it's supposed to be.
Only if you want to.
Don, I'm not going sleep with you!

Don't ask me that.
Don't do that?
You're my friend.
I like you as a friend.
That's ok, I understand.
Do I have any possibility?
In the Future, sometime down the track?
Maybe?
Maybe!
Ok, I'll take that.
I'm not going sleep with you!

I like spending these nights with you.
I'll sleep on your couch.
It's very comfortable.
I like sleeping on your couch.
But I'm not going sleep with you!

"The Don"
10.09.2020

Giulietta Masina
As "Cabiria" in Nights of Cabiria"

Books written by "The Don"

"My Life with Chickens & other stories: I Pity the Poor Immigrant"
Published:
10th September, 2019
Autobiography Book 1:
0 – 12 years old

"Poems for Misfits, Miscreants, Misanthropes, Mavericks, Losers & Malcontents!"
Published:
10th June, 2020
Book of Poems 1

"Poems for Troubled Minds & Trouble Hearts"
Published:
10th August, 2020
Book of Poems 2

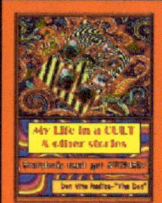

"My Life in a CULT & other stories: Everybody Must Get STONED!"
Published:
10th September, 2020
Autobiography Book 2:
15 – 30 years old

"Poems for Restless Minds & Restless Hearts"
Published:
10th October, 2020
Book of Poems 3

"Poems for Anarchists, Revolutionaries, Outlaws & Dissidents!"
Published:
10th November, 2020
Book of Poems 4

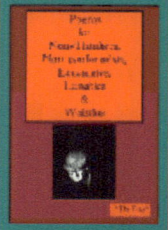

"Poems for Non-Thinkers & Eccentrics"
Published:
10th December, 2020
Book of Poems 5

"The Rantings of a Madman"
Published:
10th January, 2021
Book of Poems 6

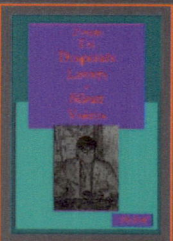

"Poems for Desperate Lovers & Silent Voices"
Published:
10th February, 2021
Book of Poems 7

"Poems for Tormented Minds & Tortured Souls"
Published:
10th March, 2021
Book of Poems 8

All available ONLY online